Color Library Travel Series

AMERICA

Designed and Produced by
Ted Smart & David Gibbon

MAYFLOWER BOOKS · NEW YORK CITY

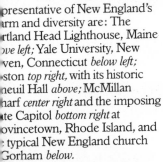

representative of New England's arm and diversity are: The rtland Head Lighthouse, Maine ove left; Yale University, New ven, Connecticut below left; ston top right, with its historic neuil Hall above; McMillan harf center right and the imposing te Capitol bottom right at ovincetown, Rhode Island, and typical New England church Gorham below.

dramatically illuminated
American Falls, part of spectacular
Niagara Falls in New York State,
can be seen *below left,* and *left* the
'Maid of the Mist' at the base of
Horseshoe and Niagara Falls.
Shown *below right* is the Art Deco
top of the Chrysler Building amid
New York's inimitable skyline, seen
beyond Brooklyn Bridge *above right;*
above the statue of Atlas on Fifth
Avenue, and *below* the Statue of
Liberty.

The resplendent White House *above r*
and majestic Capitol Building *right* are
among the many fine monuments in t
nation's capital, Washington D.C. *Abo*
is shown the Barnegat Lighthouse on t
tip of Long Beach Island, New Jersey;
left the Assembly Room in Independe
Hall, Philadelphia, and *below* the Natio
Cemetery in Gettysburg, Pennsylvani

Picturesque houses and shops
right and carefully restored
buildings, such as the T-shaped
Courthouse of 1770 *left,* recaptu
the atmosphere and appearance
of Colonial Williamsburg's 18th
century existence. St. Michael's
Episcopal Church in Charlestor
South Carolina is pictured *belou*
and *above* the glittering skyline c
Memphis, Tennessee.

Shown *above* is the magnificent Sternwheeler steamer 'Natchez' as plies the muddy waters of the Mississippi at New Orleans, Louisi *left* Civil War cannon and *below* a commemorative statue in the Vicksburg National Military Park, Mississippi, and *right* the impressiv skyline of Atlanta, Georgia, by nigl

...ulous Florida has so much to
...r – sophisticated Miami *left*; the
...ctacular Seaquarium *bottom right*,
...its performing seals and dolphins
...killer whales *below*, and
...hanting Walt Disney World, with
...airytale Cinderella Castle *above*,
...orful squares *right* and much-loved
...ney characters *top right*.

...Walt Disney Productions.

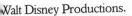

Shown *above* is North Lake Shore Drive; *left* the Regency Hyatt O'Hare Hotel and *below* the dazzling skyscrapers of Illinois' Chicago, on the southern shore of Lake Michigan. *Below left* can be seen Detroit, Michigan; *right* a typical farm in the rolling pastureland of Iowa, and *above right* Cincinnati, Ohio, connected to Covington Kentucky, by a series of bridges.

Pictured *above* is the State Capitol of St. Paul, Minnesota and *top left* its downtown area beyond the Marina, and *left* 'Gateway Arch,' Jefferson City, Missouri. *Far right* can be seen the notorious old mining town of Tombstone, with its unfortunate 'Claim Jumper' *right; bottom left* Columbia Pictures' Old Tucson; *below* Phoenix, and *above right* the Civic Center of Tucson, in the rugged state of Arizona.

Revealing Arizona's muted
grandeur are: *above left* Canyon
de Chelly; *left* Moran Point,
and *above* Hopi Point in the
Grand Canyon; *below* Cathedral
Rock in Sedona's Oak Creek
Canyon, and *right* the majestic
Painted Desert.

The Pueblo, in the picturesque New Mexico community of Taos, is pictured *above left,* and *above* Oklahoma City. *Right* can be seen the pink granite Capitol of Austin, and *below left* Freeway 59, part of Houston's elaborate road system *below,* in the prosperous state of Texas.

Majestic Hidden Lake at Logan Pass, Glacier National Park, Montana is shown *left;* beautiful Maroon Lake *above,* and *right* the old ghost town of Sneffels, near Ouray, in scenic Colorado, and *below* Texas' famous landmark, The Alamo, at San Antonio.

Cosmopolitan San Francisco, with its
Fisherman's Wharf *above left,* colorful
'Chinatown' *below left* and charming cable
cars *below* is, like Los Angeles, the City
Hall of which can be seen *above* beyond
the Civic Center Mall, one of California's
most famous cities. One of L.A.'s many
attractions, 'The Queen Mary,' moored at
Long Beach, is shown *above right,* and
below right fun-loving Las Vegas, Nevada.

Oregon, a state unsurpassed in its variety
of lavish scenery and unspoilt ocean
beaches *above right,* is also noted for its
majestic mountain scenery, evidenced in
Mount Baker *left,* Mount Hood *below* and
Mount Jefferson *right,* in the superb
Cascade Range, while perched on a
headland overlooking the restless Pacific
surf is the Heceta Head Lighthouse *above.*